Collins

KEITH WEST
UNSOLVED MYSTERIES

Contents

Introduction	2
A ship without a crew	3
The Loch Ness monster	8
The Bermuda Triangle	14
The mystery of Stonehenge	18
The lighthouse keepers of Flannan Isle	24
The man who stepped into the future	30
The man who could escape	
f|	34
	40

Introduction

Has anything ever happened to you that you couldn't explain?

This book is about the strange things that sometimes happen: about odd events in puzzling places; about sightings of weird creatures; about planes, boats and people that have disappeared without a trace.

We think we understand most of what happens in the world, but some things are still a mystery — a mystery that we can't solve.

A ship without a crew

Imagine seeing a ship sailing across the sea with nobody on board! That's what happened in the strange story of the *Mary Celeste*.

The *Mary Celeste* was a small sailing ship that carried cargo across the Atlantic. In early November 1872, she left New York, bound for Italy, with nearly two thousand barrels of pure alcohol aboard. The captain had his wife and little daughter with him, plus a crew of seven men.

On 4 December, a British ship saw the *Mary Celeste* drifting off the coast of Portugal. Some of her sails had been torn by the wind.

As they drew closer, the captain of the British ship shouted, "Ship, ahoy!" Nobody answered.

Two men were sent to board the strange ship.

It was creepy on the deck. The only sounds were the creaking of wood, sails flapping and a barrel rolling back and forth.

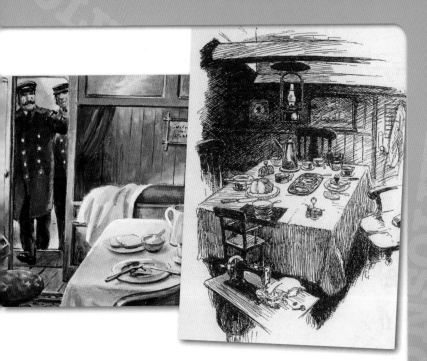

In the captain's cabin, they found a half-eaten breakfast on the table and clothes and toys scattered all over the floor. A pillow on the bed was still marked by the shape of a child's head.

The clock had stopped. The ship's sailing record ended suddenly on 25 November. Everyone seemed to have left the ship in a hurry.

The captain and the crew had left their money, sea boots and pipes.

The captain seemed to have taken the instruments and charts needed to find his way at sea. A hatch over the cargo was left open. The lifeboat had gone, and a frayed rope trailed from the ship.

The crew of the British ship decided to sail the *Mary Celeste* into harbour, hoping to get a reward.

Investigators tried to find out what had happened. Had the sailors turned against the captain? Or had pirates attacked the ship? There were no signs of fighting …

One possible explanation was suggested. Perhaps the cargo of alcohol had begun to give off fumes in the hot sun. There was a danger it could explode, so everyone had rushed to the lifeboat.

They had tied the lifeboat to the ship. But the rope had broken and the boat had drifted away. Then rough seas had swamped the lifeboat, drowning everyone on board.

That is only one theory. We may never know what really happened on the *Mary Celeste*.

The Loch Ness monster

Does a strange monster live in the depths of Loch Ness?

The loch is a vast area of inland water in Scotland. It is nearly twenty-four miles long and is very deep in places – about twice as deep as the North Sea. It is a strange and powerful place.

The sightings

The monster, known as Nessie, first became famous in 1933 when a photograph claiming to show the creature was published on the front page of the Scottish *Daily Record* newspaper.

Yet as far back as the seventh century, there have been reports of a "dragon" or "water horse" shaking itself in the lake.

Since then, many people claim to have seen the monster. More photographs of Nessie have been taken, including one that showed up on Google Earth in 2009.

The sightings all describe the monster as looking like a very large reptile or eel, with a long neck, small head and several humps on its body.

But let's take a closer look at the evidence. Here is the 1933 *Daily Record* photo.

There were several reported sightings in 1933 and 1934, including the photo opposite.

In 1951 a photo of three huge black humps was taken.

Then, in 1960, a strange object was captured on video moving across the water.

The theories

Many theories have been suggested. Could the photos show not a monster, but perhaps …

- a tree root brought to the surface

- a large diving bird

- or even an elephant from a passing circus taking a morning swim?

Were any of the photographs tricks, as one photographer admitted on his deathbed?

Could the strange splashes and bubbles be caused not by Nessie's movements but by earthquakes beneath the loch?

Or … is it possible that there really is a huge reptile living in the depths?

Organisers of a swimming event at the loch in 2005 clearly took the rumours seriously. Before the race, they insured the swimmers against monster bites. Any swimmer who was bitten by the monster would get up to £1 million! Of course nobody was attacked.

Searching for Nessie

Despite many searches, no hard and fast proof has yet been found.

In 1969, Dan Taylor, an American submarine expert, searched the loch but found nothing, although he did claim to have been bumped by "something large at the bottom of the loch".

Operation Deepscan in 1987 was the biggest attempt to find the truth. Small boats swept the loch from one end to the other while scientists used the latest **sonar** (sound) technology to search its depth.

Three contacts were recorded with something thought to be larger than a seal. Could this have been Nessie?

One thing is for certain: this isn't a mystery the Loch Ness tourist industry want solved any time soon …

The Bermuda Triangle

The Bermuda Triangle is the name given to a strange area of the Atlantic Ocean.

It is also known as the "Triangle of Death".

A surprising number of ships and planes have disappeared in this small area of ocean. It is thought that more than a thousand lives have been lost here. Most of the disappearances – more than one hundred – have taken place since 1945.

Not a single body has ever been found.

US coastguards holding a box of life jackets, the only remains of a huge tanker that went missing in 1963.

Here are just two of the things that have happened.

Flight 19

In 1945, five US Navy aeroplanes flying through the area reported that their instruments were going haywire. Then all communication was lost. A rescue plane was sent out, but that too lost contact and was never heard from again.

Did you know?

One of the crew had refused to go out because he'd had a feeling something bad was going to happen.

The crew of Flight 19

15

The one who got away

In 1964, an airline pilot was on a routine run across the Bermuda Triangle. Suddenly, he noticed a strange glow at the tips of the wings – a glow that got stronger and stronger until he could hardly read the instruments. Then the instruments went totally out of control. The glow was almost blinding.

He had almost given up when the glow started to fade. The instruments began to work again and he could take control of the plane.
It was a lucky escape …

Other reports talk of the sky turning yellow and the sea looking very odd.

Many theories have been suggested:

- sudden tidal waves caused by earthquakes

- fireballs from the sky

- a time-space warp leading to another dimension.

But can these theories explain what the pilots saw? What do you think?

The mystery of Stonehenge

Every year at sunrise on the longest day of the year, thousands of people gather at a group of gigantic stones.

This is Stonehenge.

Today, visitors to Stonehenge find a mix of standing and fallen stones. Looking up at these monuments from long ago, visitors ask themselves many questions.

Who built the stone circle?

When did they build it?

How did they build it?

And, most of all, **why** did they build it?

When was Stonehenge built?

By studying the stones that form Stonehenge, scientists have worked out that it was built in three phases, starting over five thousand years ago.

Phase 1: Bodies were buried at the site.

Phase 2: The ditch and bank around the site were dug and a timber frame was made.

Phase 3: Blue stones were dragged from over one hundred miles away, to create the first circles. These stones were later moved around and much larger stones were added.

How was Stonehenge built?

There are no written records to answer any of the other questions about Stonehenge.

Exactly **how** it was built is a mystery. The stones are huge and weigh several tons each. We know that some of them were brought a long distance from the area we now call Wales.

The wheel had not been invented at this time, so the stones can only have been moved by water, on huge rafts, and dragged on sledges by many men. Some experts have worked out that moving even some of the stones must have taken about fifteen hundred men working for ten years!

The three phases of building probably needed more than thirty million hours of work!

Even with modern cranes, the large stones are difficult to move.

Why was Stonehenge built?

This is the biggest mystery of all. Here are two of the many theories.

1 Was it a temple for worshipping the sun?

The stones line up with the rising sun on the summer **solstice** or longest day (21 June).

This picture shows what the stone circle would have looked like when it was first built, as the sun rose on the longest day.

2 Was it a healing place?

The smaller blue stones were taken from areas close to "healing" springs. This might explain why it was worth carrying them so far. Many of the skeletons found around Stonehenge had injuries or bone problems. Did people come to the stone circle to find relief from their pain?

Axes from all over Britain have also been found in the ground around the stones. This suggests people came from far away to visit this special place.

There must have been an important reason for building something so large. But we may never know for certain what it was. We can only go to Stonehenge and wonder at the mysteries that surround it …

The lighthouse keepers of Flannan Isle

Have you heard of the Flannan Islands?

These islands off the west coast of Scotland are spooky places. Nobody lives on them. Local people say they are haunted by ghosts …

In 1895, a lighthouse was built on the largest island, as many ships had been wrecked in the seas around there. The lamp was first lit in December 1899.

A four-man team looked after the light. They took it in turns to rest: three stayed on the island, while one went back to the mainland.

A steamboat brought supplies to the men. It stopped offshore while a small boat went in to the landing place. A crane had been built to lift heavy goods out of the boat. The keepers then carried them up the steep steps to the lighthouse.

It was a hard, lonely life.

On 15 December 1900, after a week of storms, a passing ship reported that the light had gone out. The weather suddenly took a turn for the worse and the supply ship was unable to sail for another ten days. Only on 25 December did the weather improve enough for it to set out.

Joseph Moore, the spare keeper, was on board. He was very worried. There was no sign of life on the island. No signal flags were flying.

The captain of the steamboat blew his whistle and lit a flare. Still there was no reply.

Moore ran up the steps to the lighthouse. The gate and main door were closed. He shouted his friends' names. Nothing!

Inside, the living room was empty. There were cold ashes in the fireplace. The clock had stopped. Everything was tidy, but one chair had tumbled over. Two outdoor coats had been taken. The third was still on its hook.

Moore climbed the stairs to the great light, with the wind howling round the tower. The lamp had burnt out but nothing else seemed wrong.

The men searched the island.

The jetty with the crane was damaged. Ropes were scattered across the crane cover. They had been taken from a box kept higher up the cliff.

A huge wave must have smashed against this side of the island. Could this wave have swept the men away too?

9/1/1901

40/-
1.

4 (a)

C O P Y

Telegram from the Master, "Hesperus", to Mr Murdoch, St.Kilda,Trinity, Edinburgh.

Handed in at Callanish at 7.14 p.m. Received at 8.27 p.m.
26.12.00.

A dreadful accident has happened at Flannans. The three Keepers, Ducat, Marshall and the Occasional have disappeared from the Island. On our arrival there this afternoon no signs of life was to be seen on the Island. Fired a rocket, but, as no response was made, managed to land Moore, who went up to the station but found no Keepers there. The clocks were stopped and other signs indicated that the accident must have happened about a week ago. Poor fellows they must have been blown over the cliffs or drowned trying to secure a crane or something like that. Night coming on, we could not wait to make further investigation, but will go off again to-morrow morning to try and learn something as to their fate. I have left Moore, Macdonald, Buoymaster, and two seamen on the Island to keep the light burning until you make other arrangements. Will not return to Oban until I hear from you. I have repeated this wire to Muirhead, in case you are not at home. I will remain at the telegraph office to-night until it closes, if you wish to wire me.

Master "Hesperus".

26/12/00

In this telegram, the ship's captain suggests the men must have been blown over the cliff.

But the weather records showed that on 15 December, when the light went out, the sea had been calm.

Perhaps two of the men had gone to look round after the earlier storm. One might have slipped into the sea. Hearing cries from outside, had the third man jumped up, knocking over his chair and forgetting his coat? Had all three somehow fallen into the sea and been swept away?

Other people had different ideas. Did one man go mad and kill the others? Or had they been turned into the three large, black birds seen on the island?

Their bodies were never found and the mystery lives on …

The man who stepped into the future

Many people have disappeared, but not many people reappear – except perhaps Rudolph Fenz.

The story goes that he disappeared from a small American town in 1876. He was described as a kind man, loved by his family and friends. There was no reason for him to go missing.

The American police searched everywhere, but he was never found. His family and friends waited for him to return – but he never did.

Fast forward to 1950. A man was hit by a car near Times Square in New York and killed. When police looked at the body, they noticed he was dressed in rather old-fashioned clothing.

According to the police, the man was wearing a black coat, a wide-brimmed hat, narrow trousers and buckle shoes. These items were all worn in the late nineteenth century.

In the man's pockets, the police found a bill for the upkeep of a horse and carriage. He was also carrying a letter postmarked 1876 and some shiny coins from the same year.

Stranger still, they found a calling card in the man's pocket bearing the name … Rudolph Fenz!

Rudolph Fenz

FIFTH AVENUE, NEW YORK, NEW YORK

Could Fenz have turned up seventy-four years after he had disappeared, without having aged at all?

The police handed the Rudolph Fenz case over to the Missing Persons investigators.

They discovered that Ruldoph Fenz had a son named Rudolph Fenz, Junior. Fenz, Junior had died a few years earlier, but his widow was still alive. She told them her husband had been four years old when his father disappeared. She showed them an old photograph of Rudolph Fenz, Senior. He looked exactly like the man killed near Times Square.

Could the story be true? Did Rudolph Fenz really step into the future?

Could a person really travel through time?

The man who could escape from anything

Harry Houdini was a magician who claimed he could escape from anything.

His career began in an American circus in 1891. Before long, he was making money by escaping from locked chains.

One day, Houdini asked two policemen to handcuff him. As they watched, he freed himself.

A London theatre company was so amazed that they booked him for six months. Soon, Houdini was touring the world. He became known as the "Handcuff King".

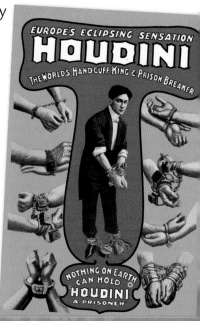

EUROPE'S ECLIPSING SENSATION

HOUDINI

THE WORLD'S HANDCUFF KING & PRISON BREAKER

NOTHING ON EARTH CAN HOLD **HOUDINI** A PRISONER

How did he do it?

Houdini studied locks all his life. He knew how every type of lock worked. Sometimes he'd have a key tucked up his sleeve and sometimes he'd open locks by using a shoestring. Once, he even escaped from a prison transport van!

Sometimes Houdini would hang from a rope tied very high up, in full view of everyone. He always managed to break free and survive!

Playing with death

Houdini was popular because people knew his stunts were dangerous. There was always the chance something could go wrong.

Once, he was hung upside down in a locked glass and steel cabinet full of water. His ankles were clamped. To escape, he had to hold his breath and find a way to free himself.

Another time, Houdini was buried alive. Something did go wrong on that stunt and he only just survived. He hadn't realised how heavy soil could be!

How did he really die?

Ask people how they think Houdini died and they'll probably say one of his tricks went wrong. Two Hollywood films show Houdini dying as he tried to escape from a locked steel cabinet. In fact, he escaped without harm every time.

Another theory is that he was poisoned. Houdini had made enemies by trying to prove that **mediums** were frauds. A medium had upset Houdini by saying she had spoken to his dead mother.

Houdini with one of the mediums he thought was a fraud.

mediums

people who claim to speak with the spirits of the dead

In fact, doctors at the time of his death said that Houdini had died from appendicitis, aged 52. He had refused to see a doctor until it was too late, because he would not stop his show.

But no **autopsy** was ever performed on his body and the rumours about his death continue to this day.

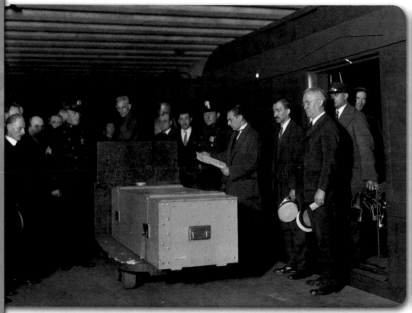

Houdini in his funeral casket.

autopsy
when doctors open up and test a body to find the cause of death

David Blaine is sometimes called the present-day Houdini. Like Houdini, he is a magician who performs amazing feats. Perhaps you remember seeing him on television when he was shut inside a glass box above the River Thames in London. He stayed there for forty-four days, with only water to drink.

He has also been buried alive and survived under water for seven days and seven nights!

Flying saucers

In June 1947, a rich American was enjoying a flight in his private plane. Suddenly, he saw nine strange, large objects flying below him. They were brightly lit, flat and shaped like saucers. They flew very fast.

Later, he wrote about what he had seen and drew some pictures. Not long afterwards, two airline pilots also saw nine fast-moving discs.

Soon, newspapers were full of stories about "flying saucers". Some even published photos.

This photo was taken in America in 1952.

These reports were not the first.

In 1878, an American farmer claimed to have seen a large, dark, circular object flying above him "at wonderful speed".

In 1904, some American naval officers in the Pacific saw three bright-red, egg-shaped objects flying together. They suddenly changed direction and raced away into space!

In 1926, an American pilot reported "flying man-hole covers" moving past him. And in the same year, someone in Tibet saw in the sky "something big and shiny … moving at great speed".

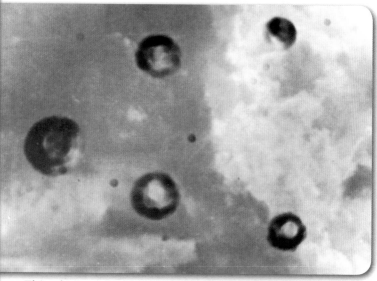

This photo was taken in Ireland in 1950.

What could these **Unidentified Flying Objects** (or UFOs) be? Were they secret flights or weapons being tested? Or maybe balloons, clouds or meteors? Did people just imagine they had seen these things? Were any of the photographs tricks?

Governments looked into these strange sightings. Most UFOs could be explained away, but a few remained as mysteries. Could they be visitors from outer space?

The Roswell Incident

Some people think that an event in 1947 proves that UFOs come from other planets. A farmer in Roswell, New Mexico, in the USA, reported that a strange craft had crashed at his ranch. Airmen from a local air-force base came to look.

At first sight, the wreckage seemed to be nothing out of the ordinary: it was like a large military balloon with a radar disc hung underneath. And that seemed to be the end of the matter.

But, thirty years later, one of those same airmen told a very different story. The remains, made of a strange metal, were in fact from a flying saucer. Four bodies had also been found. They were said to be aliens! One had been found alive.

He said the Air Force had hidden all the evidence and kept it top secret.

The military looked into the case but denied his claims. Ever since, the rumours about the Roswell flying saucer have continued.

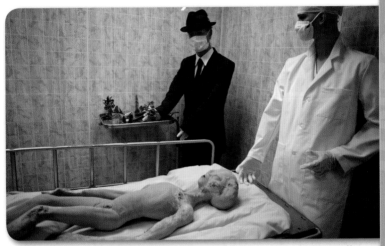

In 1995, film of an alien autopsy at Roswell came to light. It turned out to have been made using plastic dummies like this one.

Keep looking at the sky. Perhaps you, too, will see a glowing disc flying above you. Where has it come from? Where is it going? Who might be inside? And, if it is from outer space, do you *really* want to find out … ?

Reader challenge

Word hunt

1 On page 7, find a verb that means "flooded".

2 On page 21, find a noun that means "flat boat".

3 On page 41, find an adjective that means "round".

Story sense

4 What kind of man was Rudolph Fenz? (page 30)

5 What evidence was there that Fenz turned up seventy-four years after he had disappeared? (pages 31–33)

6 What different reasons were given for Houdini's death? (pages 37–38)

7 According to the farmer's report, what happened in the Roswell incident? (page 43)

8 What was different about the story the airman told years later? (pages 44–45)

Your views

9 Do you think the way the author tells the stories of the mysteries makes them sound believable? Give reasons.

10 What do you think really happened in the Roswell incident? Give reasons.

Spell it

With a partner, look at these words and then cover them up.

- evidence

- notice

- surface

Take it in turns for one of you to read the words aloud. The other person has to try and spell each word. Check your answers, then swap over.

Try it

Read page 16 again. With a partner, imagine one of you is the pilot "who got away" and the other is someone who doesn't believe in mysteries. Tell them your story and try to persuade them it's true.

William Collins's dream of knowledge for all began with the publication of his first book in 1819. A self-educated mill worker, he not only enriched millions of lives, but also founded a flourishing publishing house. Today, staying true to this spirit, Collins books are packed with inspiration, innovation and practical expertise. They place you at the centre of a world of possibility and give you exactly what you need to explore it.

Collins. Freedom to teach.

Published by Collins Education
An imprint of HarperCollins*Publishers*
77–85 Fulham Palace Road, Hammersmith, London W6 8JB

Browse the complete Collins Education catalogue at **www.collinseducation.com**

Text by Keith West
© HarperCollins*Publishers* Limited 2012

Series consultants: Alan Gibbons and Natalie Packer

10 9 8 7 6 5 4 3 2 1
ISBN 978-0-00-748890-2

British Library Cataloguing in Publication Data.
A catalogue record for this publication is available from the British Library.

Commissioned by Catherine Martin

Edited and project-managed by Sue Chapple

Picture research and proofreading by Grace Glendinning

Design and typesetting by Jordan Publishing Design Limited

Cover design by Paul Manning

With particular thanks to Christopher Martin and Sue Chapple.

The publishers do not endorse or present as fact the stories and theories in this book.

Acknowledgements

The publishers would like to thank the students and teachers of the following schools for their help in trialling the Read On series:

Southfields Academy, London
Queensbury School, Queensbury, Bradford
Langham C of E Primary School, Langham, Rutland
Ratton School, Eastbourne, East Sussex
Northfleet School for Girls, North Fleet, Kent
Westergate Community School, Chichester, West Sussex
Bottesford C of E Primary School, Bottesford, Nottinghamshire
Woodfield Academy, Redditch, Worcestershire
St Richard's Catholic College, Bexhill, East Sussex

The publishers gratefully acknowledge the permission granted to reproduce the copyright material in this book. While every effort has been made to trace and contact copyright holders, where this has not been possible the publishers will be pleased to make the necessary arrangements at the first opportunity.

The publisher would like to thank the following for permission to reproduce pictures in these pages (t = top, b = bottom, c = centre, l = left, r = right):

p 3 Keystone/Getty Images, p 4r, 5l, 6 & 7 © Look and Learn/The Bridgeman Art Library, p 4 Mary Evans Picture Library/Alamy, p 5 Mary Evans Picture Library/Alamy, pp 8–9 Lian Deng/Shutterstock, p 10 Trinity Mirror/Mirrorpix/Alamy, p 11 Keystone/Getty Images, p 12 Popperfoto/Getty Images, p 13b John Dee/Rex Features, p 13t Rex Features, p 14b © Bettmann/CORBIS, p 15 Time & Life Pictures/Getty Images, pp 16–17t R.L.Hausdorf/Shutterstock, pp 16–17b delreycarlos/Getty Images, pp 18–19 Durden Images/Shutterstock, p 20 Pecold/Shutterstock, p 21 Fox Photos/Getty Images, p 22 DEA PICTURE LIBRARY/De Agostini/Getty Images, p 23 Robert Harding World Imagery/Alamy, pp 24–25 Ian Cowe/Alamy, p 25 Stephane Bidouze/Shutterstock, pp 26–7 Zacarias Pereira da Mata/Shutterstock, p 28 National Records of Scotland, NLC3/1/1/40 page 9, Telegram from Master, lighthouse tender, "Hesperus", to Mr Murdoch, St Kilda, Trinity, Edinburgh reporting accident at Flannan Isle Lighthouse, 26 Dec 1900, pp 28–29 Luisa Puccini/Shutterstock, p 30t Time Life Pictures/Mansell/Time Life Pictures/Getty Images, pp 30–31 SuperStock/Getty Images, p 32t George Bailey/Shutterstock, P 33 photo by Rex Features (1733991l), p 34 & 36 Buyenlarge/Getty Images, p 35r Mary Evans Picture Library/Alamy, p 35l FPG/Getty Images, p 37 Hulton Archive/Getty Images, p 38 (c) Bettmann/CORBIS p 39 JIM WATSON/AFP/Getty Images, p 40 Mary Evans Picture Library/Alamy, p 41 Popperfoto/Getty Images, p 42 Keystone-France/Gamma-Keystone via Getty Images, p 43 Sipa Press/Rex Features, p 44 UNITED STATES AIR FORCE/AFP/Getty Images, p 44 Jason O. Watson/Alamy.